THE WORLD OF
Baby Animals

THE WORLD OF
Baby Animals

BRYAN HODGSON

HUGH LAUTER LEVIN ASSOCIATES, INC.

Copyright © 1995 Hugh Lauter Levin Associates, Inc.
Editor and Photo Researcher: Leslie C. Carola
Designer: Ken Scaglia
Editorial Researcher: Katherine Ozment
Copy/Production Editor: Deborah T. Zindell
ISBN 0-88363-795-2
Printed in Hong Kong

Frontispiece: *Fishing is a deep subject for this young grizzly bear cub, which follows its mother into Naknek Lake to learn about migrating salmon in Alaska's Katmai National Park. Although primarily vegetarians, grizzlies and other brown bears depend on salmon to store up fat for the long winter hibernation.*

Title page: *In Antarctica, an Emperor penguin chick emerges from a sheltering fold of skin and feathers, where it was hatched from an egg balanced for weeks on its father's feet while its mother hunted for food.*

Page 6: *Adult Gentoo penguin feeds its chick in Antartica.*

CONTENTS

To Erla

INTRODUCTION

A newborn elephant calf (above) finds its feet in a forest of friendly legs.

Sunset silhouettes a family group of elephants heading toward a water hole in Kenya's Amboseli National Park. Long hunted illegally for their ivory tusks, elephants now receive heightened protection thanks to African leaders who heeded warnings that these magnificent creatures were threatened with extinction. Researchers have discovered each elephant family has its own character, with personality types ranging from benign to bossy, irritable to docile. All unite in defending and caring for their young.

If you were fortunate enough to watch a band of elephants coming at sunset to drink from a desert water hole in Namibia's Etosha National Park, you would witness one of the grandest spectacles in nature. These huge animals proceed with surprising grace, shifting their weight easily from side to side, almost silent except when they blow occasional trunkfuls of dust to ward off troublesome insects. The sun turns the dust clouds into a brilliant veil, silhouetting the animals like some golden dream of the days of creation.

Trotting confidently amid this multitude of giants, several juvenile elephants earn an occasional nudge from a solicitous trunk when they venture too closely underfoot. These precocious youngsters, with faces that seem somehow to smile, convey the unmistakable impression that this is a family outing, with parents and young joined amicably with uncles and aunts and cousins in a pleasant ritual.

Family? Scientists have no hesitation in using the word to describe the social habits of elephants. The community life of these largest of land mammals is one of the most stable and enduring in nature. Mothers undergo a two-year gestation period before delivering their 250-pound babies. In their difficult and painful birth, they are usually

Mother moose licks one of her newborn calves as it tries out its legs in Denali National Park, Alaska. Moose youngsters grow rapidly on a rich diet of mother's milk and soon learn how to thrust their heads completely underwater to graze on succulent acquatic plants.

Secure in mother's shadow, a young polar bear cub surveys its brand new icy world. Some day the cub will learn to hunt for seals and fish. But for now, he will feed on super-rich mother's milk for up to 18 months before being sent off on his own.

attended by two females that ward off predators. Mothers will nurse their calves for up to four years. Elephant mothers share caretaking chores, often nursing each others' calves while the mothers are off feeding themselves. Males will fight to protect their harems and drive off post-adolescent male offspring to protect against inbreeding.

By contrast, the lowly house mouse, which can produce fifty to seventy young in a season, will wean her brood of six babies in three weeks or so to make room for the next batch. The wildebeest foal, born on the open African veldt, will be licked clean and must be on its feet ready to follow its mother within a few minutes of birth.

For all mammals, regardless of their size or environment, the first period of touching, tongue-washing, and nursing are crucial to the infants' physical and cognitive development. Deprived of these by loss of a mother, young animals frequently display symptoms of anxiety and fear which affect their ability to survive and procreate in later life.

To help insure that these profound needs for nurturing are met, nature provides newborns with a powerful armament. Along with the elemental instinct to thrust and cry for mothers' milk, they possess the charming faces, comic awkwardness, and playful behavior that trigger the mothers' equally profound instincts to care for, enjoy, and protect their broods. Certainly, these animal babies trigger warm and affectionate feelings in humans—one reason, perhaps, why so many naturalists, photographers, and artists have devoted their lives to studying and recording the behavior of animal families.

However tender the scenes of nurturing and play, they are merely the relative calm before the many conflicts and hazards of life. Predators such as lions, cheetahs, and wolves must be taught the bloody business of hunting. Grazing and browsing animals like deer and antelope need little help discovering what's good to eat, but must be taught to spot danger and react instantly. Playful combat among

*On the open grasslands of
Africa, a newborn wildebeest
calf is nudged to its feet
immediately after birth and is
ready to run from predators
within hours.*

infant males is merely practice for the violent and often fatal battles
they must undertake for dominance—nature's way of insuring that
the strongest genes are passed down the generations.

For the most part in these critical preparations for life, mother knows
best. Among mammal species, only three to four percent of fathers
participate in the feeding and educating of their offspring. Among the
most noteworthy in this regard are wolves. Male wolves have been
observed caring tenderly for their pregnant mates, and both parents
share hunting chores, feeding their young by regurgitating partly
digested prey. By contrast, American bobcat mothers do all the hunting for their broods, and react savagely against visits by the fathers
of their young, knowing instinctively that the male parent may
threaten and even kill his offspring.

Protecting their young awakens in mothers the most profound and
powerful instinct of all. When danger threatens, females can erupt in
such elemental fury that they frequently intimidate predators much
larger and better armed, and often sacrifice their own lives as well.

In recent years, scientists like America's Diane Fossey and Britain's
Jane Goodall have employed their unique perspectives in the study
of gorillas and chimpanzees, primates that are classified—along with
humankind—as anthropoids. Through years of observation, they
have described complex primate societies in which males play strong
roles not only as procreators, but also as protectors and providers.

Although fathers are observed playing and interacting with their
young, it is the mothers that play the crucial role. Chimpanzee babies
aren't weaned until they are five years old, and they stay with their
mothers until they are between nine and fourteen years old. Mothers
show what looks very much like love for their offspring, and orphans
frequently are adopted by other females. The young will sometimes
grieve their mother's death with every evidence of despair, displaying
throughout their lives the signs of what can only be called depression

A white tail fawn rests beneath rhododendron blossoms in a North American woodland where its mother has hidden it while she forages for food. Instinctively, the fawn will lie low in absolute silence.

and antisocial behavior. There are dark aspects in this prehuman world. War and murder and infanticide have been observed, as well as cannibalism.

Primate behavior contains clues to human behavior. The study of primate emotions is considered valuable because behavior develops very rapidly, and animals have no way to mask feelings. Perhaps one of the most poignant animal pictures ever taken was that of a baby rhesus monkey gazing beseechingly into the glassy eyes of a terry cloth dummy which was the only "mother" it had ever known.

When all is said, one thing remains comfortingly clear. The study of infant creatures, animal and human alike, is an affirmation of human-kind's most crucial survival instincts.

These need no scientific names, nor any justification.

They are simply affection, understanding, love of life, and hope.

A wide-eyed harp seal pup watches for its mother in the wintry Gulf of St. Lawrence. Its white juvenile coat, designed by nature as camouflage, was a fatal attraction to hunters who once clubbed them by the thousands for the fur trade. Public revulsion has almost completely ended the annual hunt.

With the greatest of ease, an orangutan mother cradles her baby on her stomach as she makes her aerial way through the Malaysian forest on the island of Borneo. Orangutans use their feet like a second set of hands, and seldom descend to the ground. Babies rapidly develop a tight grip on their mothers' fur.

Bold patterns of light and dark fur help hide a cheetah cub from danger in Masai Mara Nature Reserve in southwest Kenya. Soon this furry camouflage will help the cheetah to stalk its prey.

A grey wolf pup relaxes in summertime warmth outside its family den in Montana. Soon it will join the pack as a novice hunter.

What's this? A three-month-
old grizzly bear cub inves-
tigates new buds in a wintry
landscape. Although a true
carnivore, the grizzly also
dines on buds, berries, and
other vegetation.

Baby raccoons seem ready for
mischief at the entrance to their
hollow log home. Raccoons,
cousins to the bear family,
can survive as efficiently in
suburban gardens as they do
in the wild.

Triple threat to predators, triple treat to the eye, triplet baby skunks stay close for comfort in a field of yellow blossoms. Cousins to otters and wolverines, skunks help keep rodent populations in balance.

No threat to anyone, but destined to become a canny survivor, a wild burro colt stands on the threshold of life in Custer State Park, South Dakota.

A cheetah cub seems ready to
begin its own hunting career
in Masai Mara Nature
Reserve in southwest Kenya.

An orangutan mother and
baby cuddle together sharing
a moment of repose in the
Borneo forest.

CARE AND FEEDING

In the first moments of life, infant mammals are helpless. Blind and naked, or tottering on uncertain legs, they need instant care and feeding and protection. In one of the most universal and profoundly moving scenes in nature, their mothers respond immediately, washing and caressing the youngsters and nudging them gently towards the mammary glands which will feed them milk containing the rich blend of proteins, fats, vitamins, minerals, and antibodies necessary for life and growth.

Photographed in an exquisite moment, a mother deer and her fawn symbolize the ever-renewed tenderness and tenacity that wild creatures devote to rearing their young. Such intimate contact creates a bond of scent and voice that will keep the pair together for the critical months of dependency.

A cheetah mother gazes indulgently at her three-week-old brood in southern Kenya. Her cubs will stay with her for as long as two years, learning how to hunt.

A koala bear cub clings tightly to its mother's back on a nighttime foraging excursion looking for tender eucalyptus leaves in Lone Pine Park at Brisbane, Australia. Looks can be misleading: the koala has a violent temper, and, when disturbed, can use its tree-climbing claws as weapons.

A grey kangaroo joey rides comfortably in its mother's pouch. Australia is the home of most of the world's marsupials, which represent a stage of evolution between egg-laying creatures and true mammals.

These milk glands are thought to have evolved from sweat glands millions of years ago, when animals began the slow evolutionary change from laying eggs to gestating their young within their own bodies. Marsupials like America's opossum and Australia's kangaroos, wallabies, koalas, and duck-billed platypus are examples of the half-way stage in that evolution. After birth, their half-formed fetuses, less than an inch long, crawl into pouches on their mothers' bellies. There they stay for several weeks until they have completed their initial growth and are ready to explore the world outside. The platypus represents the earliest stage of mammalian evolution. Milk is secreted through scores of glands in the mother's skin, which her infant licks while securely nestled inside her pouch.

Even these primitive creatures have vastly different lifestyles, and nature tries to insure the survival of the tiny, helpless offspring by adapting female anatomy to the individual baby's needs. Mother kangaroos possess large pouches in which their infant joeys can ride comfortably long after weaning while she bounds rapidly along on powerful hind legs. The koala, which spends a lot of time crawling up and down trees, developed a marsupial pouch that opens downwards to make it easier for their newborn to crawl inside. When the baby emerges several months later, it rides on its mother's back.

For all mammals, the first days of life are fraught with dangers, both from predators and the environment. In response, the animals have evolved many protective strategies. For instance, before giving birth an American cougar locates not one den, but two, the second being a refuge to which she'll move her cubs if danger threatens. On the African veldt, where there's no place to hide, the wildebeest and other ungulate (hoofed) herd-dwelling species give birth standing up. For giraffe babies, that means that birth comes as something of a shock: they drop some five feet to the ground—apparently with no ill effects! Immediately after birth mothers lick away the birth fluids, an act that must be a reassuring gesture for the newborn, but more importantly teaches mother and baby their unique scents by which they can recognize each other instantly amid a herd of others. Within

Tall and tender, a giraffe mother licks birth fluids from her newborn. Able to browse the high branches of trees, giraffes have no need to compete for food with shorter animals.

Grizzly bears once were known as ursus horribilis *by scientists, who were truly terrified by their great height and implacable hostility to anything that threatened their cubs. Now known more sensibly as* ursus arctos, *a mother and cub share a peaceful moment in an Alaskan spring.*

five minutes to an hour, the calves are ready to follow the herd and run from predators if necessary.

The birth process of the American buffalo, or bison, is remarkably well-adapted to its environment. The large shaggy bovids can purposely suspend birth during savage spring blizzards, sparing their newborns from exposure to fatal cold. By contrast, domesticated cattle descended from animals imported many years ago from Europe have no such instinct, and often require 24-hour-a-day obstetric assistance from ranchers. The ultimate strategy may be that of bears, which give birth in their fortresslike dens during their winter hibernation and barely awaken for feedings.

Whales and dolphins are born underwater. Blue whale babies are the largest on earth—some entering the world at twenty-five feet long. Large or small, youngsters are quickly nudged to the surface so they can learn to breathe through blowholes on top of their heads. Then they dive below and, like any other mammal, instinctively nurse. Hippopotamuses, which are true amphibians, are born in rivers or lakes. Baby hippos can nurse anywhere—ashore as well as under-water. Thick-skinned as they are, baby hippos are prime targets for crocodiles, and so they swim close to their mother's shoulder for as long as a year.

Although fur seals and sea lions are also water-dwelling mammals, they spend their first days of life on the beaches, rocky shores or ice floes where they are born. Mothers "haul out" of the water to give birth and feed their calves. The milk of fur seal and sea lion mothers is particularly high in fat, which the babies can store up for several days while the mothers return to the sea to hunt for food.

In the Bering Sea, fur seals return by tens of thousands to give birth on the spot where they were born on the Pribilof Islands or Russia's Kommandorsky Islands. Soon after giving birth to a pup conceived in the previous season, the females will mate again. Their pups grow rapidly and soon venture out to sea with their mothers for on-the-job

Grizzly bear mothers nurse their cubs for as long as two years, as this one is doing in Alaska's Denali National Park. When weaned, grizzlies enjoy a mixed diet of berries and other vegetation, but they also fill up on salmon and occasionally warm-blooded prey.

training in hunting squid and fish. By the time mating season ends, the youngsters are ready to survive on their own.

One of the most endearing marine mammal pups is the Pacific sea otter. Born ashore, it soon learns to swim, and nurses by climbing aboard its mother, who floats on her back. Would-be predators—including man—soon learn that the sea otter's tender appearance masks a savage protective instinct and teeth that can bite like bolt-cutters.

There is no one prescribed age for weaning among mammals. Among grazing animals like zebras and bison, mothers conduct a sort of movable feast for the first few months, and as long as the youngster can keep up with the herd it is allowed to nurse at will. If separated from its mother, a newborn calf's distress cries will be heeded, but gradually the calf learns to graze for itself, and the mother actively discourages efforts to nurse, usually at the onset of the mating season.

The higher the social development of a particular species, the longer a maternal relationship persists. Porcupines leave the nest within a few days—perhaps ejected by the mother because babies quickly develop formidably sharp quills. Young rats must fend for themselves by the age of three weeks or so. Virginia opossum babies, usually born in litters of about six, are fed by their mother for about three months, and then the brood literally cling to their mother's back as she moves about until they can fend for themselves.

Among predators, whose complex lifestyles require much learning, weaning takes place naturally as mothers—and occasionally fathers—return from the hunt and begin to feed their youngsters by regurgitating partially digested meat. For the most part, big cats give birth and raise their youngsters in isolation. Lions are the exception. Their kittens are particularly privileged, living out their juvenile days in family groups called prides, protected and nursed not only by their mother, but also by three or four females that babysit while mothers hunt. Reality sets in when they are allowed to tag along on

A *huge humpback whale tends
its youngster shortly after
birth. Newborns must be
boosted to the surface to take
their first breath before they
can nurse. When grown,
humpbacks feed by straining
krill and small fish through
the curtainlike strands of
cartilage called baleen that
line their huge mouths.*

31

On the grassy beach of South Georgia Island in the southern hemisphere, an elephant seal pup seems to smile in contentment as it snoozes, waiting for its mother who is off to feed herself so she can provide the large quantities of rich milk her youngster needs.

hunts, when they quickly realize they have to compete for food not only with their parents but with hyenas and vultures as well.

Grey wolves have a particularly tight-knit family structure. Packs of up to fifteen animals form and are strictly ruled by a dominant male and a dominant female. Only one female becomes pregnant each year, producing up to half a dozen pups. This striking control of the birth rate has developed as a response to the limited prey within the pack's territory. Naturalists have estimated that to sustain life one adult wolf requires more than a dozen deer every year. Only those who have learned to hunt successfully will survive. Wolf pups are particularly precocious and begin pouncing on insects, lizards, and small frogs soon after birth in preparation for the adult roles they must play.

Baby gorillas, orangutans, and chimpanzees inherit the highest social patterns of all and are treated in ways strikingly similar to human practices. Even though youngsters soon understand that they can find edible vegetation and fruit for themselves, they are nursed and cuddled by their mothers for as long as five years, and a deep attachment continues long after weaning. The instinct to "mother" is found throughout the family, and sometimes the mother's older daughter will help care for a new infant. Chimpanzees "grow up" by around age twelve, at which time they can become parents themselves. In some baboon families, a young adult male will "adopt" an immature female, and groom and care tenderly for her for up to a year in what seems to be very much like an engagement period before mating.

One of the most striking facts of life that humans can learn from mammal families is that maternal skills are paramount. A baby's development and ability to survive is dependent for the most part on its mother's skills. Babies with nervous and irritable mothers become nervous and ineffective themselves, and stand less chance of surviving in what can often be a cruel and deadly grownup world. Strong and caring mothers bring up confident young. In other words, like mother, like daughter—and, like mother, like son!

On the rocky shore of Alaska's Walrus Island, hundreds of male walruses rest after days at sea. Soon they will be battling for the right to mate—battles that ensure the strongest genes will prevail.

(Overleaf) Elephant seal pups share a quiet bay with a large nesting colony of king penguins on South Georgia Island in the southern Atlantic Ocean. Bleak as they may seem, such islands offer vital shelter from the fierce storms that whirl around the continent.

A brilliant color scheme of black and white makes all zebras seem the same, but in reality the stripe patterns are as unique as human finger-prints. Here a Grant's zebra takes her newborn for a training run.

A mother elephant shields her calf from the noonday sun at Lake Nakuru National Park while cattle egrets feed on insects disturbed by the pair.

A wolf mother and her pup search for food on a game ranch in Montana. Hunted and poisoned almost to extinction by cattlemen and sheep ranchers, the wolf has somehow managed to survive, and now is being reintroduced in Yellowstone National Park.

Like the wolf, the cheetah is also near extinction, but this large cat is now protected in Africa. In Tanzania, a mother watches her brood get their first taste of meat, feeding on a Thompson's gazelle she has brought down.

Migrating salmon provide a sumptuous repast for grizzly bears, which must store up body fat for the winter. Mother bears bring their enthusiastic cubs along to teach them how to fish.

On South Georgia Island in the southern hemisphere, a gentoo penguin treats its downy-feathered nestling to a regurgitated fish meal. In a month or so, the youngster will sprout its own sleek black-and-white feathers and be ready to hunt. Penguins spend most of their lives at sea, and come ashore only to mate and raise their young.

In Africa, a lion cub gains a
strong sense of security from
playful body contact with its
mother. As it grows up, it
will spend its adolescence in
equally close contact with
other youngsters of the pride.

Getting close for comfort in
the Borneo forest, a baby
orangutan gains a vital sense
of confidence and identity
from its mother, and will stay
with her for years until
reaching maturity. Unlike
many other primates,
orangutans do not form
groups, but live in relative
isolation until mating time.

A two-tone tapir mother and her striped youngster live in a dense Malaysian forest, where they search in the undergrowth at night for tender new plant shoots. With no fur to protect them from sunburn and insects, tapirs spend much of their time in water.

Pouncing in pursuit of a small reptile, a spotted cat known as a serval is most at home in wetland areas of southern Africa. Unlike most wild cats, it can adapt readily to areas colonized by humans.

If these emperor penguins appear to feel proud of themselves and their youngster, they have earned the right: all three have survived weeks of savage cold on the ice at Cape Washington, about 225 miles south of McMurdo Station, the United States main Antarctic research base.

No less proud than the penguins but considerably warmer, a mother hippopotamus escorts her hefty youngster along a muddy lake shore in Kenya. Weighing up to a ton, hippos are most comfortable afloat or strolling submerged on lake bottoms.

COMMUNICATION

Safe from hazards of the wild is the Hanuman langur (above), honored as a sacred animal in India. Nevertheless, mothers cuddle and guard their youngsters against a sometimes frightening world.

Making good time through low-growing Alaskan shrubs, three young moose obey their mother's direction as they hustle out of harm's way in Denali National Park. Twins are common among moose, but rare triplets create an extra burden of parental anxiety when wolves or grizzly bears are on the prowl.

R UN! NOW! There's no question what the fleeing mother bear means as she snarls furiously at her three cubs, which have paused to look up at the Russian helicopter approaching their den in the forests of Kamchatka. Immediately the cubs turn and scamper after her into the trees. What sound did she make? How did the cubs know its meaning? There is no way for those aboard the helicopter to know. But split-second observation convinces them that urgent mother-cub communication has taken place.

Baby animals must learn survival language early in life. Zebras, those optical illusions of the animal world, may recognize mothers by stripe patterns as well as scent. White-tailed deer and baby rabbits learn to run for cover when they see adults flash the white underside of their tails—a silent warning that danger is near. Prairie dog pups may learn a three-tone warning system—a whistlelike call to signal that hawks or buzzards are about, a barking noise that indicates a land predator is near, and an "All-clear" signal that says it's once again safe to play just outside the mouth of the family burrow. Beaver kits dive to the underwater entrance to their lodge when an adult smacks the water with its tail. In other animal groups, a sudden silence can send a message. Some grazing animals seem to be constantly gossiping with each other as they move along, but freeze to attention and become ready for instant flight when one of them spots danger and stops grunting.

Nowhere is animal communication so elaborate and so fascinating as within families. Ethologists have found that wolves strategically place drops of urine around their trerritory— olfactory signs which say "No Trespassing." Within the family, body language tells who's who: dominant wolves walk with tails and heads high and ears alert; lesser pack members carry heads and tails parallel to the ground; outcasts slink around with flattened ears and their tails between their legs. These roles are communicated during puppyhood, when playful battles actually serve to produce dominant or submissive behavior in males and females alike. Among all the world's canines, one puppylike communication is unmistakable: with forepaws outstretched, hindquarters elevated, and tail waving like a flag, they say, "Let's play!"

To humans, the howling of wolves and coyotes lends an eerie loneliness to the stillness of the night. But the animals, from puppy to adulthood, seem to enjoy these choruses for a variety of reasons. Adults may be affirming territorial claims, or announcing a search for a mate; early in the morning hungry pups may simply be sending a wake-up call. Wolf and coyote pups have another "feed me" signal: they will lick or nip at the face of their mothers or other caretakers,

A zebra stripling stands close to its mother, and reveals the subtle differences of pattern that enable them to recognize each other by sight.

Howling in harmony, three grey wolves in Bayern, Germany, may be telling their canine neighbors that trespassers aren't welcome, or may simply be celebrating their survival in a world whose human inhabitants are becoming increasingly hostile to animal predators. Wolf families are close knit, but dominance struggles to determine status in the group begin early in each pup's life.

Enjoying a moment of relaxation, a Thompson's gazelle still keeps a watchful eye out for predators in Serengeti National Park, Tanzania. Unlikely as it may seem, these sleek antelope are related to other animals whose hooves possess two toes, such as the hippopotamus, the pig, and even the American buffalo.

Recognizable by the shape of its parenthesis-like horns, a mother topi (also known as a sassaby) nudges her newborn up on his shaky long legs. On the grasslands of Kenya, herds of up to 15,000 animals sometimes congregate during migration. The young must be ready to keep up with the herd, or perish.

prompting the adults to regurgitate food. In Africa, observers have noted that primates carry through to adult courtship a practice similar to the infant ritual in which the male pretends to feed his prospective mate, who adopts a childish pose. Some believe this form of communication may have been the origin of what humans call kissing!

Chimpanzees can be rowdy chatterboxes at times, but spend far more time quietly grooming each other, holding hands, gazing into each others' eyes, or responding to each other with facial expressions that range from outright hilarity to shy smiles or fang-baring rage. Baby monkeys delight in gazing at the world upside down between their legs, and delight even more when playful adults will join in. The young are confident exploring such a diverse world if they know they can retreat to a maternal embrace that says, in effect, "Don't worry!"

On the plains of Africa, where baby animals are prime targets for predators, herds of grazing creatures like wildebeest and zebras seem to share with each other knowledge gained from experience. Babies are all born at about the same time, to ensure that at least some will survive to breed. The youngsters then follow the herd, which is often led by females who will vary behavior depending on which predators are present. They will move close to a pride of lions, apparently knowing that these predators pose no threat for days after a kill. Likewise they seem untroubled by cheetahs, apparently knowing that this fastest of feline predators runs out of gas after a relatively short chase. But experience has taught herds to stay well clear of wild hunting dogs, which are not speedy runners, but which can keep up a deadly chase for many hours.

One of the most spectacular forms of communication may be that of the Thompson's gazelle and the springbok, who even as youngsters perform stiff-legged high jumps called "stotting" or "pronking." Scientists are uncertain whether these jumps signal the presence of danger, or are designed simply to discourage predators from continuing the chase. Others think they may be an expression of the sheer joy of being alive.

Swift, untimely death for grazing animals means a rich and robust life for lions, which of all the big cats maintain the most elaborate family life, forming prides composed of several females and one or two males. Newly weaned cubs are considered the responsibility of all, and they join in one hyperactive kindergarten under the supervision of young females. Here they discover the delights of chasing their own tails and those of their guardians, earning caresses, baths, and quick snacks of milk or regurgitated food. Such attentions teach the cubs that they are valued and cared for. But they are also taught respect. When cubs become too obstreperous or give in to the temptation to try out their new claws, elders will administer a cuff to the ears, or pick the unruly cub up by the scruff of the neck and give it an admonitory shake. Even in the best of families, somebody has to be the boss.

Nowhere is mammal communication more direct and to the evolutionary point than in the battles that males of many species fight to establish domination. With thunderous head-butting or the rattling clash of huge antlers, animals such as sheep and elk continue an eons-old struggle to decide which males will be able to pass along their seed. Body language proclaims the outcome: while losers trudge away in obvious defeat, the winners approach their harems with a

Kissing cousins on the sub-Antarctic island of South Georgia, two elephant seal cubs get to know each other while their mothers hunt at sea. When grown, elephant seals exhibit a characteristic called dimorphism, meaning that males grow to be three times the size of females and weigh as much as four tons.

Spotted dolphins cruise gracefully in the warm and limpid waters of the Bahamas. Like many toothed cetaceans, dolphins seem to take a particular interest in human activities. In turn, humans are fascinated with the cetacean's elaborate vocabulary of squeals and squeaks with which they communicate underwater.

proud strut that clearly announces their superiority. But there's often a price to be paid for victory. Next year's babies may never see their fathers, for many males spend so much energy mating and fighting that they often lose weight and body fat and may be unable to survive a severe winter.

No such fate seems to await fur seals in the Bering Sea, where dominant bulls preen and pose and roar with such imperial dignity that many young males resign themselves to bachelorhood and don't even bother to come ashore. Females, on the other hand, come ashore in droves to give birth to babies conceived a year earlier, gathering around the bull to send seductive signals of their renewed readiness for mating.

Of all the marine mammals, whales and dolphins have been the most difficult to observe in nature. Dolphins in captivity, however, seem to delight in communicating with humans. In recent years, researhers have been allowed to swim in the open ocean with tight-knit dolphin family groups and listen to their continuing chorus of clicking noises and elaborate songs. Some of the sounds are like sonar waves, striking remote objects and returning echoes which the dolphin can use to navigate or locate prey. Some bursts of high frequency sound may be so intense that it can stun or kill fish and other sea creatures. And some sounds may be as-yet-untranslatable messages from an ancient and very intelligent species to a very young and still somewhat immature family of mammals called Man.

Known for traveling in highly
disciplined troops, baboons
have developed powerful
methods of communication.
Here, a group of mothers
appears to be consulting
about child care.

In Kenya, a cheetah mother
placidly tolerates the antics of
her kittens. Later she will
teach them to be more polite,
and pass on the serious
lessons of survival.

Elephants love mud because it protects their thick but very sensitive skin from sunburn. At a mud hole in Kenya, a protective mother keeps her calf from getting in too deep.

The call of the wild? Or the yawn of the wild? Either way, this leopard cub seems very much at home in a Kenya tree, knowing that its mother will respond instantly to signals of distress.

The peaceable kingdom will
be a very temporary affair
for this pair of youngsters,
one a wolf pup and the other
its natural prey, a mule deer
fawn.

Nose to nose, a young harp
seal exchanges reassuring
messages with its mother, who
has returned to her breathing
hole in the ice after a hunting
trip near Magdalen Island
in Quebec Province, Canada.

PLAY

High spirits and high jinks go together as a young zebra kicks up its heels while traveling with its kinship group. Tens of millions of animals must take arduous journeys each year to find water and forage as dry and rainy seasons alternate. Today, as Africa's human population grows, living room is gradually shrinking for the vast free-ranging herds—much as it did in America during the 19th century, when mighty buffalo herds were reduced to near extinction.

Two grey wolf pups act out the combat roles they will take more seriously when such behavior determines which animals become leaders of the pack.

High spirits and high jinks go together as a young zebra kicks up its heels while traveling with its kinship group. Tens of millions of animals must take arduous journeys each year to find water and forage as dry and rainy seasons alternate. Today, as Africa's human population grows, living room is gradually shrinking for the vast free-ranging herds—much as it did in America during the 19th century, when mighty buffalo herds were reduced to near extinction.

Two grey wolf pups act out the combat roles they will take more seriously when such behavior determines which animals become leaders of the pack.

We all take delight in watching a kitten pounce playfully on moving bits of paper or string. But you shouldn't be surprised sometime later when that same cat begins to bring home real mice, large insects, and small birds. Despite many thousands of years of domestication, feline pets are born with feral instincts fully intact. House kittens share with their wild cousins the ability to develop formidable hunting skills by playfully ambushing their brothers and sisters, cuffing vagrant leaves, or diligently stalking their mothers' twitching tails.

Childhood is a time for play, and this mountain orangutan baby strikes a charmingly awkward pose as it follows its mother through the maze of branches and vines in a Malaysian forest.

The days of childhood last much longer for elephants, such as for these two youngsters splashing and squirting each other in an African water hole. They will stay close to their mothers for as long as four years before being fully weaned. Young adult females will stay with the herd, but young males are driven away to start families of their own.

But are these playful mammal babies really having fun? Many scientists doubt it, believing that all animal behavior is genetically programmed for survival. Frisky calves butt heads only to prepare for the adult battles of the mating season. Fraternal squirrels chasing each other up and down trees with death-defying speed are simply practicing for future mating rituals. Wolf pups engaging in mock combat are merely in spring training for contests that will establish the pack's future hierarchy. And cheetah cubs chasing each other around scrub bushes are only developing muscles for future 60-mile-an-hour sprints in pursuit of dinner.

Nevertheless, even the most pedantic scientists will have difficulty suppressing a smile while observing animal youngsters' comical behavior—even if they believe that a smile is actually an instinctive survival gesture designed by nature simply to awaken maternal instincts or avoid aggression.

It's not hard to imagine that playful colts and cubs, foals and calves, kittens and pups are reacting exuberantly to self-discovery in a brand new world, much as a human infant rapturously discovers its own toes. Adult mammals frequently share a little of the rapture too: how else to explain a huge old male gorilla solemnly tickling a baby gorilla with a flower? Or a mother elephant squirting trunkfuls of water at her calf?

But sooner or later playing does evolve into training, with parents showing youngsters how to earn their living at a time when mistakes won't be dangerous or fatal.

All young animals have a lot to learn, but young grizzly and brown bears have especially interesting discoveries ahead when it comes to food. Following their mother for as long as three years, they sample a wide variety of edible leaves, roots, berries, bugs, and occasionally a dead deer or elk. They learn to climb trees for safety, with a parental cuff on the rear end if they're not quick enough, and then make the belated discovery that climbing down a tree is a lot harder than

Fraternal scuffles will give way to solitude when polar bear cubs mature at the age of 18 months. By then they will be fully trained in the art of hunting seals and fish, their main diet in Earth's most hostile climate.

By contrast, these Alaskan brown bear cubs view the catching of migrating salmon as a delightful game. Although fish is a vital part of the brown bears' pre-hibernation diet, they feed mostly on berries and low-lying forest vegetation.

climbing up. Gorging themselves on wild honey, they find that bee-stings really hurt. In summertime, watching their elders snagging migrating salmon, they gallop into rushing streams to find that amateur bears aren't always a match for muscular and determined fish. All these lessons must be learned in time to put on weight for winter hibernation.

Among canine predators, puppies get an early start. Adult wolves will playfully ambush youngsters, and then allow them to tag along on hunts at three months of age. Occasionally an adult will step on a pup and hold it down, a playful gesture which biologists feel may duplicate that used by adult males and females to affirm rank within the pack.

Foxes hunt by night and teach pups how to find rodents and frogs by sound and scent as well as sight. In coyote families, which are strongly united, fathers will bring home live mice or other small animals and allow youngsters to practice catching them. Sad to say, hyena pups occasionally get the earliest start of all. They have exceptionally sharp incisor teeth that keep growing throughout their lives. While their mother is away hunting, fraternal play inside the den sometimes turns by accident or instinct into fratricide.

More often than not in the animal world, "family" means mother and young. Unlike lions, which lead a rich communal life in prides composed of one or two males, several females and their cubs, many species of large cats tend to be solitary except for a brief period during mating season. Cheetah mothers raise their babies alone, teaching them how to put their blazing speed to work on such prey as antelopes. Lacking the sharp claws possessed by other cats, the huntress first swipes her quarry's hind legs from under it like a cowboy roping a calf and then clamps her jaws on the unfortunate animal's neck. She allows her yearling cubs to learn other lessons for themselves, like the discovery that not only do warthogs have one of the nastiest tempers—and certainly one of the most terrifying countenances—in all of Africa's Serengeti Plain, they also have little respect for amateur spotted cats.

70

Mother makes a powerful playmate for this young Indian tiger, who will soon begin learning that silent and skillful stalking must precede pouncing successfully on prey. Survival will also depend on successful avoidance of human poachers who place a higher value on a tiger's skin than on its life. Only a few thousand survive in the forests of East Asia and the Russian Far East.

In America, parental habits of big cats vary. Bobcat babies, distinguished by devilish little tufts of hair on the tips of their ears, may know their fathers only as the surly creature their mother drives away with bared fangs and horrendous noises. By instinct she seems to know that he may try to harm his offspring. On the other hand, the male American lynx is known to bring home mice, birds, and other small animals for his family.

It is among primates and monkeys that play and learning continues the longest, sometimes to the point where it is difficult not to believe the animals have reached the level of conscious thought. Some thirty years ago, ethologist Jane Goodall discovered that chimpanzees knew how to peel leaves from a small branch, thrust the stick into a termite mound for a minute or so, and then withdraw it with a load of tasty termites aboard. Some years later scientists in West Africa watched chimp mothers teach their young how to crack nuts with stones, not merely by bashing the nuts, but by using careful strokes that left the nutmeat intact. In Japan, scientists studying a troop of monkeys called macaques watched one of them discover a way to clean sand from stalks of wheat by tossing them in water, waiting for the sand to fall off and sink, and then retrieving the floating grain. Within months, they reported, all members of the troop had learned the same trick.

Whether or not primates can reason, even on the most primitive of levels, is a question more for philosophy than science. It is certain, however, that mothers try to tutor their young. When orangutan babies learn how to swing from branch to branch the mother shows them by example which limbs are safe. It's a necessary lesson: more than 30 percent of some orangutan groups suffer broken limbs in falls. Not all primate mothers are good teachers. In chimpanzee groups, some are nervous and impatient, and bring up youngsters who have difficulty playing and socializing. Mothers who bestow generous affection, nursing, and grooming tend to produce young that are unafraid, curious, and eager to enter into group activities.

Tree-climbing is a great game for this young leopard, but when the sun goes down it will watch silently as its mother lies in ambush and then leaps from a high branch when an unsuspecting antelope, hare, or monkey passes by. After the kill, leopards take their prey back to the tree and dine at leisure, safe from would-be scavengers. By the time this youngster is a year old, it will be hunting for its own food.

It is underwater that images of play as pure pleasure become irresistible. Nudged into the sea by their mothers, baby seals and sea lions soon learn to wheel and dive with their elders in a maritime ballet unequalled for speed and grace. Speed and agility are critical skills. The babies will soon have to fend for themselves by catching fish and the elusive squid, which jet-propels itself for short distances at blinding speed by ejecting bursts of water from its mantle. Some three years later when the females reach maturity and males have noisily sorted out the matter of dominance, their underwater ballet becomes a tempestuous mating pas de deux.

At sea, when young whales hurl themselves into the air and splash down mightily, they are said to be trying to shed parasites from their skin. But somehow they convey an irresistible image of plump youngsters doing a cannonball dive from a springboard. And then there are dolphins, whose babies seem to be born with the urge to fly as well as swim. Joyously surfing on the bow wave of a ship, or leaping from the water in glistening arcs, playing with every evidence of delight, they are doubtless bent on some instinctive quest, and only coincidentally gladden the human heart.

Baby chimpanzees can become successful adults only by learning from their mothers and cousins over the 4-year period it takes them to mature. Long considered the most humanlike of primates, the chimpanzee has been used in medical research on diseases that afflict humans. In captivity, scientists have found, the offspring of caged chimpanzees lose their ability to relate to their own species, and become more dependent on humans.

The orangutan is the only large primate that customarily swings its way through the forest on vines and branches, gripping with its feet as well as its hands. Each night it will bend leafy branches into a new nest, keeping its youngster cuddled closely. Often acquired as a pet, and for some indigenous tribes for ceremonial sacrifice, the orangutan has declined to a few thousand. Current logging operations in forests of the Malaysian island of Borneo are further diminishing its only home.

Humans are well-advised to give the grizzly a wide berth, especially when mothers have playful cubs to care for. Grizzlies are known as brown bears in Kodiak, the Alaska Peninsula, and the Russian Far East peninsula of Kamchatka. They lead solitary lives except in early spring, when their tracks can be seen wandering for miles over snow-covered tundra and mountain ridges as males search for mates.

Thirty tons of humpback whale goes airborne to make a thunderous splash in Alaska's Glacier Bay National Park. Scientists have concluded that this frequently observed behavior serves to shake off parasites, or stun schools of fish for subsequent feeding. Whatever the reason, it looks very much like fun. Humpbacks migrate between the Arctic and Antarctica. Like other great whales, they were almost exterminated by hunters. Even though they are now protected by a whaling ban, their future is not assured.

Silvery breath floats above a baby orca whale swimming in formation with its mother in Alaska's Glacier National Park. Growing as long as 30 feet, and armed with formidable teeth and fearing no predator, orcas are called killer whales for their skill in hunting seals, penguins, dolphins, and other whales. Orcas have been known to leap onto ice floes and knock dozing seals into the water, or drive almost onto beaches in pursuit of penguins.

Tons of fun or terrible teens? Juvenile elephants jostle each other at the awkward age when playful behavior can turn suddenly into provocation. Watchful adults know the difference when young males approach mating age, banishing them from the herd to avoid inbreeding.

Necking is a serious business as two young giraffe males in Namibia clash to determine which is fitter to mate. Although giraffes have vestigial horns, they don't butt heads, but compete by hitting each other with sideways strokes of their long necks. Their heavy hooves also make formidable weapons against predators.

(Overleaf) Moose calves go head to head in playful combat while their solicitous mother looks on. Such play mimics the real battles for dominance they will fight when fully grown.

GETTING FROM HERE TO THERE

A tiger mother (above) carries a kitten to a new den in an Indian forest. By instinct, kittens go limp when carried and make no sound.

A baby rung-tailed lemur seems to be doing some back-seat driving as its mother prospects for fresh fruit. Lemurs look rather like cats—perhaps the reason scientists named it lemur catta—*but actually are members of the primate family.*

The seemingly random movements of animals and their families from place to place are far from simple nomadic wanderings. Whether from deep-seated instinct or accumulated experience, animals respond to daily needs, emergencies or seasonal changes in highly organized ways. Mother wolves, foxes, lions, tigers, and scores of humbler creatures will suddenly pick up their offspring by the scruff of the neck and move them one by one from their birthplace to locations they consider to be safer. Groups of herd animals like bison or wildebeest may seem to be drifting casually from one grazing spot to another, but actually are organized by gender: bands of mothers and youngsters follow older females—so-called wise cows—whose instincts have been developed over many seasons of seeking the best combination of grazing and water. Males tag along on the perimeters.

Among the most organized travelers are baboons, noted for aggressive behavior like hurling stones at tourists or attacking farmers whose crops they raid. In the forest, they forage in small groups, but moving in open savannah country where there is little tree cover, they assemble and move in troops up to two hundred strong, almost like companies of infantry. Young males are assigned the "point": they scout ahead for predators and also patrol the flanks. Dominant males guard the center, where mothers carry babies on their hips or let

85

Chimpanzees and yellow baboons (opposite) find similar solutions to transporting their young while foraging for food. Many scientists now believe that constant physical closeness to their mothers in the first year of life is as vital to healthy emotional development in infant primates as it is in human babies.

them ride piggyback, and on occasion restrain wayward juveniles by grabbing their tails. Adult males bring up the rear, where attacks by stalking predators are most likely to occur.

Frequently baboons will move along with herds of grazing animals, each group helping alert the other to possible danger. For wildebeests the alliance is particularly valuable, since up to 75 percent of their young are lost to predators.

When an animal needs an extra hand the mouth frequently serves as a prime method of transportation. The African colobus monkey will carry a tiny newborn in her mouth until it is strong enough to cling to her fur. And it's certainly a solution that occurs in many other animal species that have no hands at all, including the crocodile, which will carry hatchlings from the nest and introduce them to the watery part of their habitat. Later, baby crocs sunbathe on their mother's back. Perhaps the most remarkably hospitable mouth of land, air, and ocean is the male sea catfish, which shelters hundreds of his mate's fertilized eggs in his mouth until they hatch, and even allows his mouthful of babies to stay on until they're ready to leave home.

One of the most spectacular and complicated migrations is that of the hundreds of millions of penguins which return to their birthplaces in Antarctica and its surrounding islands each spring. Their flippers make them supremely graceful swimmers and powerful hunters in the ocean, but they seem comical and awkward as landlubbers, waddling upright to build nests of stones and sticks, or tobogganing down snow banks on their bellies to reach the sea. In vast crowded colonies echoing with vocalizations and whitewashed by the birds' habit of squirting guano into surrounding nests, both parents will incubate the eggs, and both will hunt for food to bring home to their chicks. Several weeks after birth the youngsters trade their downy grey juvenile feathers for crisp black and white ones and swim off to fend for themselves. They leave behind an "empty nest" scene that's hard to describe: teeming multitudes of molting adults standing disconsolately in blizzards of their own discarded feathers, unable to

*Mother's pouch is a tight
squeeze for this well-fed joey.
Soon it will have to travel
on its own, making way
for a tiny new sibling which
already may be growing in
the pouch. Most of the world's
marsupials exist only on
the Australian continent,
which became isolated from
other land masses millions
of years ago.*

swim and hunt for food for weeks on end until their own new plumage grows.

If there's a true "easy rider" in the animal kingdom, it must be joey, the young red kangaroo. Until the age of ten months or so, these Australian youngsters can travel in pouched comfort while mother, weighing in at about 180 pounds, covers ground in twelve- to fourteen-foot jumps at up to thirty miles an hour. There is one drawback, though. To gain added speed and ensure her own survival in a life-threatening situation, the mother can eject her youngster, knowing that her pouch already contains another tiny offspring as well as a fertilized egg, or blastocyst, attached to her womb in suspended animation.

On occasion, other marsupials also carry their youngsters on adventurous rides. The Australian tree kangaroo, equipped with climbing claws, has been seen to jump some fifty feet from branch to ground. And then there's a fuzzy-eared marsupial flying squirrel called *schoinobates volans*, which can unfold a winglike skin membrane stretched between wrists and ankles, and use it to sail for one hundred feet or more from one tree to another.

America has only one marsupial, the Virginia opossum, whose habit of feigning death when approached by a predator has given birth to a notable bit of American slang, "playing possum." Her juvenile offspring sometimes look like subway riders, curling their prehensile tails around her neck and clinging for dear life to her back as she forages for food in the woods. Sadly, not all of her litter can make the commute: she may give birth to as many as twenty babies, but has only a baker's dozen of mammary glands in her pouch. Only the strongest youngsters survive to see the outside world.

What happens when animals lose the ability to move? Wildlife biologists in Wyoming's Grand Teton National Park found a disturbing answer to the question when they noticed that a herd of bighorn sheep that made their home in the Teton mountains was

Wildebeest are known from their energetic high jinks on Africa's broad Serengeti Plain. Here an young adult shows fine form as it dives into the Mara River during spring migration.

(Overleaf) Migrating wildebeest cross the turbulent Mara River in southern Kenya. Calves must learn to swim close to their mothers lest they be swept away.

inexplicably dwindling. The reason? The isolated group of one hundred sheep had lost knowledge of a traditional winter range on the west side of Tetons, perhaps because trees that had grown thickly due to fire suppression walled them off. They were also cut off from other sheep groups to the east because of concentrated human settlement in the Snake River valley. Genetic inbreeding, plus the hardship of staying on high mountainsides during savage winters, led to a poor survival rate for lambs. The solution? Some of the trees and undergrowth were cleared away, and gradually sheep from other groups were placed on the winter range and allowed to come in contact naturally with the isolated sheep, which restored knowledge of the range and also improved the gene pool.

Studying the movements of animals sometimes can seem like part science, part magic. Unfortunately, the magic can often be lost— unless you are fortunate enough to come to know people for whom human life and animal life are still part of a whole. Some of them, the Mandan, Hidatsa, and Arikara peoples, live in North Dakota on the Fort Berthold Indian Reservation. When the iron grip of winter is broken, and geese and ducks begin to hatch yellow babies that float, like animated bathtub toys, in thousands of small ponds, old people will watch them and sing a very old and simple song:

"I'm so lucky to see you again in another spring."

A flotilla of cygnets stays close to a mute swan mother on their first shakedown cruise. Introduced from Europe to grace city parks in the U.S., the mute swan now flourishes in the wild in the north-eastern states.

This little grizzly bear greets spring with an exuberant race through an Alaskan river.

ENVIRONMENT

ANTARCTICA: Ice as far as the eye can see, temperatures so cold that steel rods can become brittle as bread sticks, winds so furious that humans can be blown about like rag dolls. Surely nothing can live here! Wrong. Here's a Weddell seal, snoozing comfortably with its pup atop the ice in the middle of a blizzard. There's a blue whale and its five-ton calf, cruising in frigid waters, scooping up mighty mouthfuls of tiny shrimplike krill. And see those male emperor penguins, thousands of them, standing like ice carvings in the night, each balancing a precious egg on its feet beneath a warming flap of skin while its mate hikes a hundred miles or more across the ice to fetch food from the sea.

Half a world north there's the Skeleton Coast of Namibia: nothing to see but hundreds of miles of Atlantic surf scouring the bare bones of southwest Africa. And yet lions live in this desert, hunting seals and giraffes and ostriches and raising their families.

Elephants live here too, trekking from water hole to water hole, youngsters trotting alongside parents and learning the way. The secret? These animals know that long, dry river beds retain moisture underground from occasional flash floods. And they know that every morning like clockwork a fog forms over the ocean and drifts inland to condense like dew on sparse bushes, grasses, and trees.

Aside from the great apes, no animal has engaged the interest and affections of naturalists as much as the African elephant, which has adapted to a wide range of conditions throughout much of the continent. One reason is that these huge creatures form small family groups whose members show great concern and tenderness towards each other. Mutual care of the young is customary, and young females will take over when mothers show signs of irritation. But the elephants seem capable of profound feelings as well. In Tanzania's Lake Manyara National Park, researchers Oria and Iain Douglas-Hamilton reported an extraordinary example: a mother elephant, bleeding

Wild water buffalo such as these survive today only in the marshlands of northern India. But they have been domesticated for centuries in the Indian subcontinent and in southeast Asia, particularly for the cultivation of rice paddies.

Also found both in the wild and as domesticated herds are reindeer, or caribou, which flourish in arctic tundra regions. These hardy animals are hunted or herded not only for their meat, but also for their well-insulated winter fur.

from spear wounds, was aided by her daughter, who used the delicate "fingers" of her trunk to press dirt in the wound and then pinch the skin together. The mother survived. In Namibia, natural history photographers Des and Jen Bartlett once watched while a mother tried to revive her drought-stricken dead calf, nudging it with her foot as though trying to wake him up. She did this for three hours before turning sadly away.

America's vast prairies witnessed similar human depredation on a much grander scale. Commercial hunters almost succeeded in wiping out the buffalo, not by killing 50 million animals, but by targeting females, which had the most unblemished hides. Every bullet ricocheted down the generations, destroying calves yet unconceived. The end of the buffalo? Fortunately not. A handful of humans—ranchers, scientists, and curiosity-seekers—collected a few dozen surviving calves and adults. From the genes of only 47 of those animals have come today's buffalo herds numbering some 200,000. Now, in springtime, in national parks and grasslands, or on scores of private ranches, you can see bright red buffalo calves nursing, butting heads, gamboling amongst their placid elders. And in winter you can marvel at their ability to confront howling blizzards, swinging their mighty heads from side to side like snowplows to reach last summer's grass beneath the snow.

For many centuries, American Indians of the Plains centered much of their physical and spiritual life around buffalo, preserving their meat and hides for food and shelter, and honoring them as a Buffalo Nation ordained by the Creator to sustain humanity. Similarly, peoples of the northern latitudes centered much of their lives around the creatures that gave them sustenance. Hunters of whales erected shrines along the shore made of huge whalebones, honoring and thanking their prey. In Siberia, where the reindeer was domesticated long ago, nomadic herders tend them during annual migrations and usher in the season of slaughter with elaborate rituals. On the American continent, where reindeer are called caribou, Eskimo hunters honor their prey as the animals migrate between feeding and birthing grounds

In summertime, high in their mountain fastness these bighorn sheep in Colorado's Rocky Mountain National Park are safe from predators, who find thin air and precipitous crags and pinnacles not to their liking. But when winter comes, the bighorn must head for lower levels to obtain food.

In Alaska, a Dall sheep and her lamb pause in pristine beauty against a background of brilliant orange lichens, which provide part of their diet in winter months.

high above the Arctic Circle and the lower latitudes where tundra grasses, mosses, and lichens are more accessible in winter. Domesticated or wild, the animals have the same method of survival in winter, daintily scraping snow away with their forefeet to nibble low-growing vegetation.

In warmer months ravenous swarms of mosquitoes and biting flies literally drive the animals crazy, sending them into desperate stampedes or huddling on remnant patches of snow, which chill the air and discourage insects.

Perhaps no animals live closer to the edge than the goats and sheep that inhabit the world's mountain ranges. Notable for their spectacular horns as well as their daredevil leaps among crags and boulders, such species as the Barbary sheep, the ibex, and the markhor feed for most of the year on delicate alpine plants and lichens, grudgingly moving downhill when winters become too severe. In America, bighorn sheep and Dall's sheep occupy the Rocky Mountains and the high ground of northern Canada and Alaska respectively. In mating season, the mountains echo with the piledriver crash of males butting heads in competition for females—a process that often sends the loser tumbling to his death and leaves the winner dazed. Females use their horns only when threatened. Lambs are born on secluded ledges, and one of their mothers' main concerns is to prevent them from leaping exuberantly into space, since these youngsters seem to be under the impression that they can fly.

If animal lives seem more comfortable in the greener lands along rivers, lakes, and forests, they are still fraught with challenges. Whether browsing on branches or grazing on aquatic plants with their heads underwater, moose teach their young to be on the alert for bears or wolves. Deer with newborn calves frequently have to be on the lookout for hawks and eagles as well, as do creatures that nest in trees and earthen dens.

High-rise raccoon cubs, all of six months old, reconnoiter their woodland home from their den in a dead tree. With able instruction from their mother, they will not only become skillful foragers and hunters of small land animals, but accomplished fisherfolk as well.

Keen-eyed cheetahs spend much of their spare time in trees, scouting for game or relaxing after a successful chase.

As humans extend their settlements farther and farther into the wild, the boundaries between the habitats have become blurred. Many moose and deer are finding delectable fare in gardens and orchards. In some eastern states, deer have become so plentiful that they are considered household pests. But aside from squirrels, rats, and mice, no creature seems to have adapted so well to human habitation as that wiliest of forest-dwellers, the raccoon. With its nimble hands it can open trash cans and raid bird-feeders, sample food left out for household pets, strip fruit from trees and carrots from the earth, and, on occasion, find comfortable nests to rear its young in chimneys, attics, and barns. If troubled, it will simply pick up its cubs and move next door.

Today, with a vast technology of observation ranging from satellites and radar to supersensitive film and infrared cameras, from genetic studies in the laboratory to infinitely patient observation in the field, there is relatively little that naturalists don't know about animals. Amid this vast store of data, one fact is quite simple: life is anything but fragile. Animal parents are tenacious and adaptable and almost miraculously tough in defending their babies. Awe-inspiring dramas of procreation and survival, acted out at the bleaker ends of Earth, represent the most powerful driving force of nature: the imperative instinct within all creatures to create and protect life .

*For grizzlies, life doesn't get
any better than this: to be
a monarch of the forest,
unafraid of any creature
including man, and to wear
a coat of fur whose brown
hairs, tipped with the gray
of maturity, glisten like silver
in the autumnal sun.*

*Plump from a summertime
diet of berries and salmon, a
mother grizzly bear and her
cub walk through an early
snowstorm in Alaska's
Katmai National Park. Soon
they will curl up in a
prepared den and sleep
winter away.*

Brash ice provides good cover for a white-coated harp seal pup whose dark-skinned mother is returning from a hunting trip. Although killing young seals is prohibited by law, the Canadian government allows hunters in Newfoundland and the Gulf of St. Lawrence to hunt 50,000 adults a year, and estimates that since 1985 the population has increased by one-third to number 3 million.

Of all the Antarctic creatures, emperor penguins choose by far the most remote parts of the icecap to hatch their young. Disturbing them is forbidden by the Antarctic Treaty, which severely limits even what scientists may do to study this largest member of the penguin family.

Wearing skin like armor plate and carrying horns that can sink small boats or hoist an enemy 15 feet in the air, the black rhinoceros is a strict vegetarian, grazing on aquatic plants or low-growing shrubs by curling its prehensile upper lip around mouthfuls of fodder. Nevertheless, other African herbivores tend to avoid the rhino, particularly when it travels from water hole to water hole with its young. Most grazers intermingle on the grassy plains with little conflict.

(Above) A herd of wildebeest seems to rely on a pair of giraffes as moving watchtowers.

Satisfying a very sweet tooth, a grizzly bear prowls through a summer field of lupines to hunt for ripe berries on the McNeil River Bear Sanctuary in Alaska. Honey is another grizzly food favorite.

Smaller Alaskan denizens like the ground squirrel sample nectar from flowers, such as the fireweed, which flourishes in Denali National Park. Both grizzly and squirrel will hibernate during the long Arctic winter, the bear in a leaf-lined den and the squirrel in a cozy grass-lined burrow.

Using its trunk as a giant powder puff, an elephant dusts itself as protection from the sun and troublesome insects. An elephant uses its trunk like an arm to bring tree branches and other food within reach of its mouth. At water holes it serves as a water-pipe, and with two liplike extensions at its tip, the trunk becomes a pair of very sensitive "fingers" which can pick up small objects.

A cloud of flamingos paints
the sky over Kenya's Lake
Nakuru National Park as a
Defassa waterbuck mother
and calf pause before
approaching the lake to
drink. Named for their habit
of staying close to lakes
and wetlands, the waterbuck
often plunges into deep
water to escape lions and
other predators.

A family tree of baboons relaxes in a wooded region of Kenya. Although they sleep in trees for safety, baboons spend most of their time on the ground.

Troops often number 100 or more, tightly organized for defense as they prospect for food.

A rookery of king penguins
provides a noisy and noisome
spectacle on South Georgia
Island in the south Atlantic
ocean. Despite the crowds,
parents can recognize their
own chicks when returning
from the sea with food.
Penguins spend most of their
life at sea, coming ashore only
to mate and molt.

(Overleaf)
The end. And the beginning . . .

117

INDEX

Page numbers in *italics*
refer to photographs.

PHOTO CREDITS

All photographs from Animals
Animals/Earth Scenes.

Norbert Rosing/Oxford Scientific
Films: front cover, p. 25; Daniel J.
Cox/Oxford Scientific Films: back
cover, p. 15, 17; Johnny Johnson: p. 2,
6, 10, 29, 32, 33, 34–35, 39, 40, 41, 48,
52, 55, 58, 66, 76, 77, 78, 79, 82–83,
93, 94, 98, 103, 106, 107, 111, 112, 113,
117, 118; Betty Press: p.8; Martyn
Colbeck/Oxford Scientific Films: p. 9,
80, 114; Doug Allan/Oxford Scientific
Films: p. 3, 84, 95; Margot Conte: p.
11, 92; Terry G. Murphy: p. 12; Marcia
W. Griffen: p. 13; Ralph A. Reinhold:
p. 14; Anup and Mahoj Shah: p. 16, 22,
42, 47, 50, 53, 61, 63, 73, 89, 90–91,
105; Stouffer Productions Ltd.: p. 18,
20, 64, 71; Zig Leszczynski: p. 19, 37;
Charles Palek: p. 21, 67, 74; Adrienne
T. Gibson: p. 23, 68; W. Gregory
Brown: p. 24; Fritz Prenzel: p. 26, 27;
Gerard Lacz: p. 28, 44, 45, 72, 85, 86;
Leo Keeler: p. 30, 38; James D. Watt:
p. 31, 59; Jim Tuten: p. 36, 87; John
Chellman, p. 43; Gerald L. Kooyman:
p. 46, 109; Joe McDonald: p. 49,
96–97, 100; Peter Weimann: p. 51;
David Curl/Oxford Scientific Films:
p. 54; Bruce Davidson: p. 56–57;
Stefan Meyers GDT: p. 60; Anthony
Bannister: p. 62, 69, 99; Francis
Lepoine: p. 65; David C. Fritts: p. 70;
Konrad Wothe: p. 75; Patti Murray:
p. 81; Hans and Judy Beste: p. 88;
Margot Conte: p. 92; Robert Maier:
p. 101; Ray Richardson: p. 102;
Leonard Lee Rue III: p. 104; John
Kroeger: p. 108; Fran Allan: p. 110;
Stan Olinski/Oxford Scientific Films:
p. 115; E.R. Degginger: p. 116.